Decorative Angel

Create a beautiful three-dimensional angel. She'll add Christmas charm to your home this holiday!

Each pattern is labeled on the back. Instructions and labels should not appear on outer sides when angel is assembled. Cut on solid lines.

1. Color patterns. (The back of each pattern will tell you what you are coloring.)
2. Cut out all patterns.
3. Roll body and glue or tape side 1 over shaded area on side 2. Completely cover shaded area on side 2. 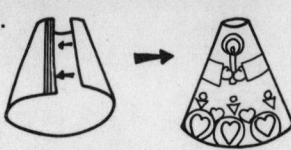
4. Cut neck on solid lines to make 8 tabs. 
5. Roll neck and glue or tape side 1 over shaded area on side 2. Completely cover shaded area on side 2. 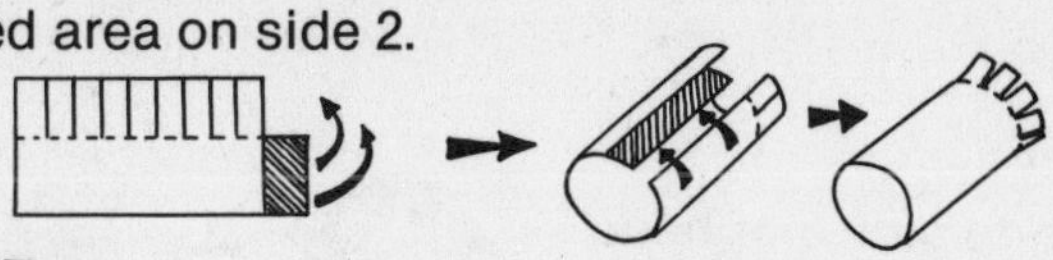
6. Bend tabs back on dotted line on neck. 
7. Apply glue to the folded back tabs.
8. Place neck inside body. Use pencil to press tabs on neck to inside of body.

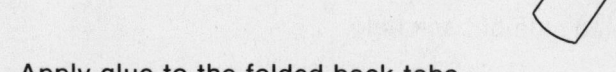

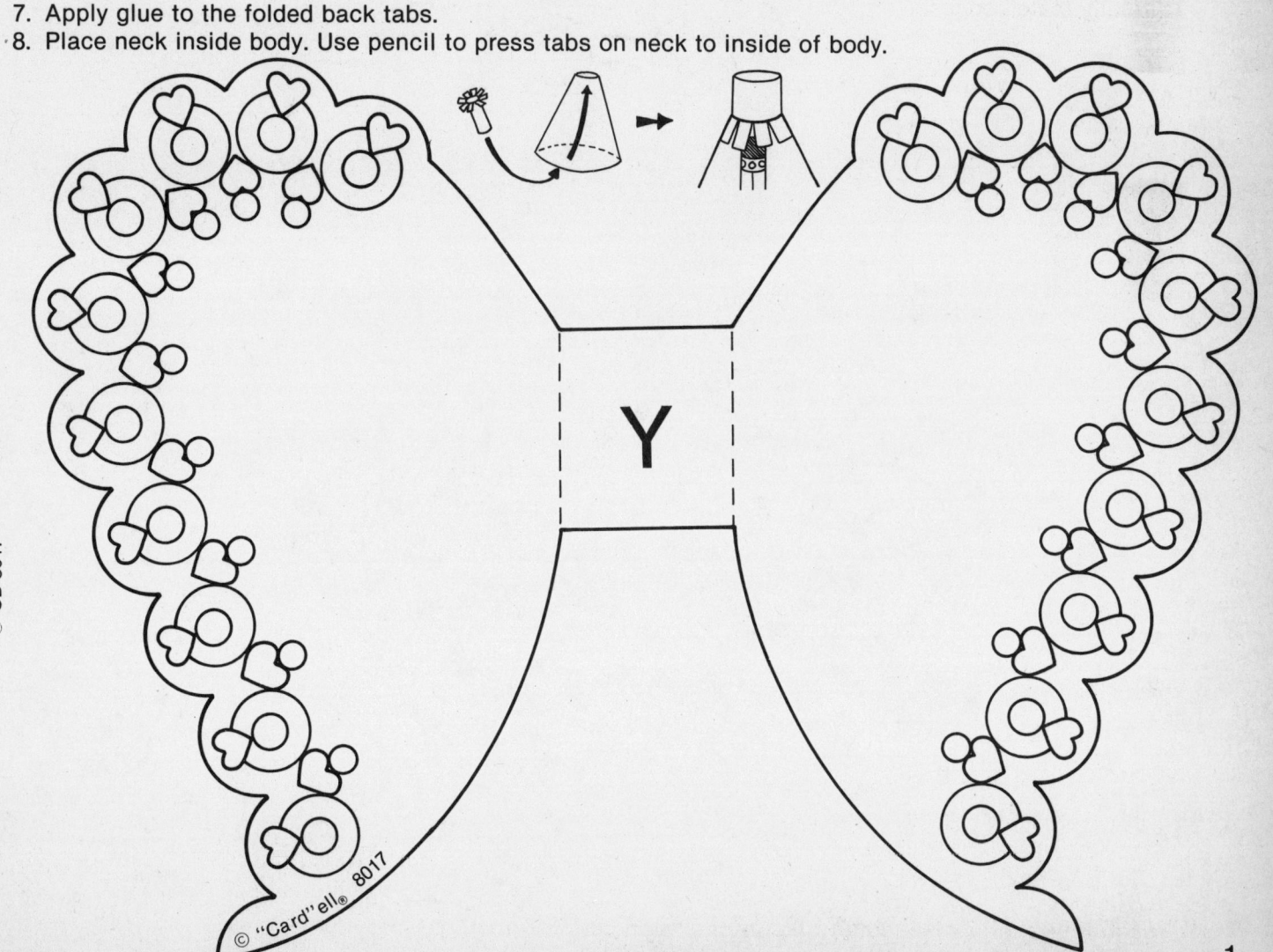

9. Cut collar on solid line and cut out inside circle.

10. Glue or tape side 1 over shaded area on side 2 of collar. Completely cover shaded area on side 2.

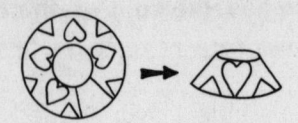

11. Slide collar over neck.

12. Fold head on dotted lines and glue or tape side 3 over side 2.

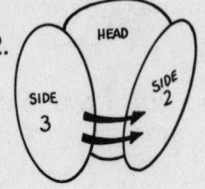

    Side 3 will completely cover side 2.

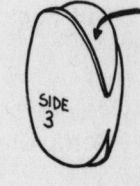

13. Glue or tape face to side 3 of head.

14. Glue or tape undecorated side of front halo to undecorated side of back halo. Carefully match edges.

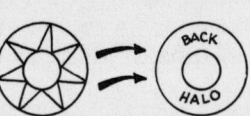

wing
A

15. Glue or tape halo to the square on the back of the head.

16. Apply glue to the front and back of the neck.
17. Slide head over neck. Make sure head faces front of body.

Cut on line to cut out circle. SIDE 2

18. Glue or tape undecorated side of wing A to undecorated side of wing B. Carefully match edges.

Use pen or pencil to punch hole, then cut with scissors.

Use pen or pencil to punch hole, then cut with scissors.

© CD-8017

3

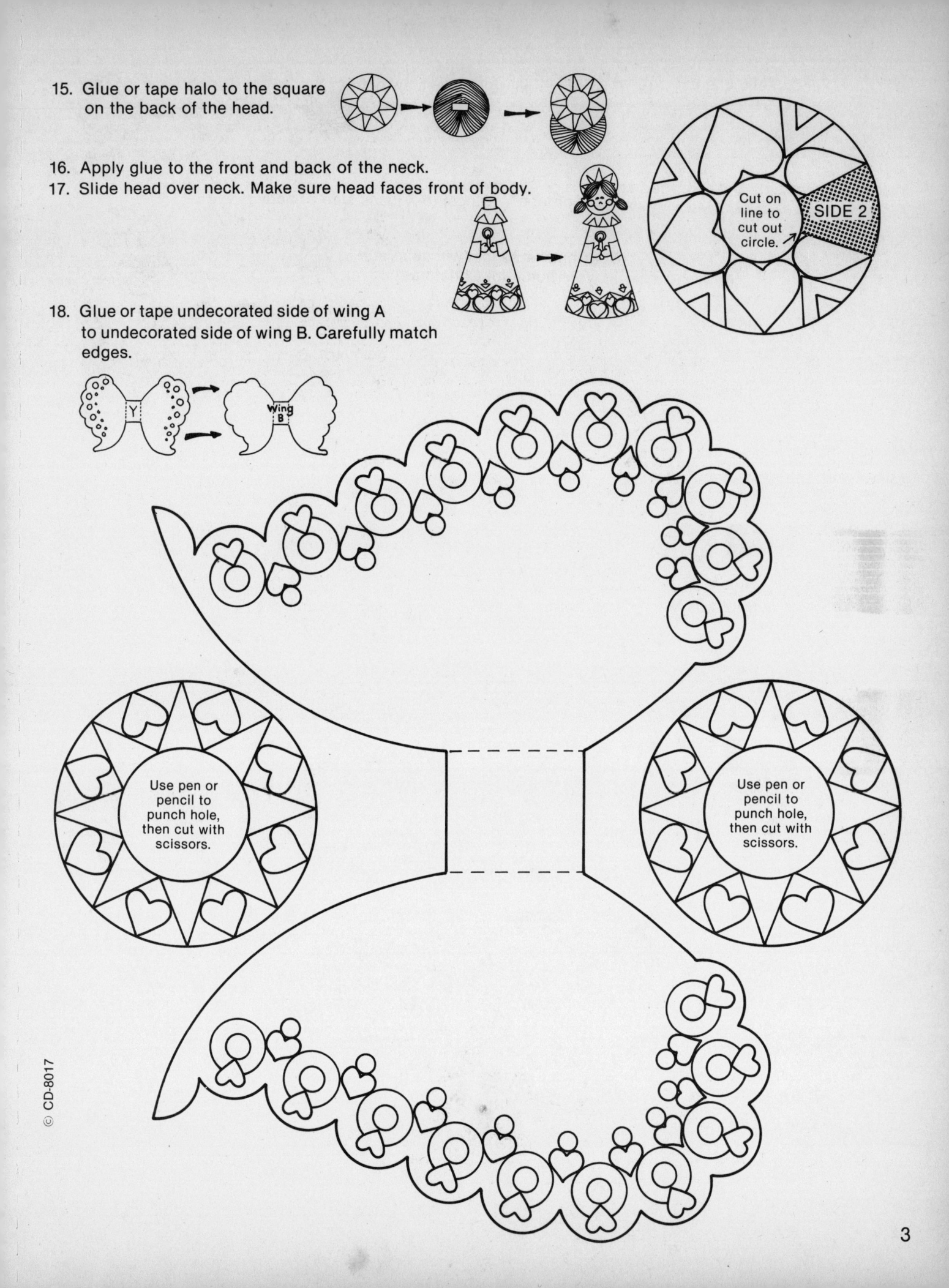

19. Fold wings on dotted lines away from Y.

collar

20. Glue or tape Y (wings) to X (back side of body.)

side 1

Your finished angel will decorate your home for Christmas!

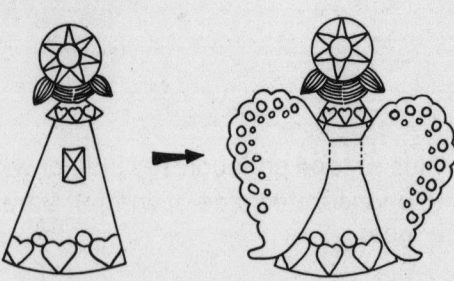

© CD-8017

front halo

wing B

back halo

4

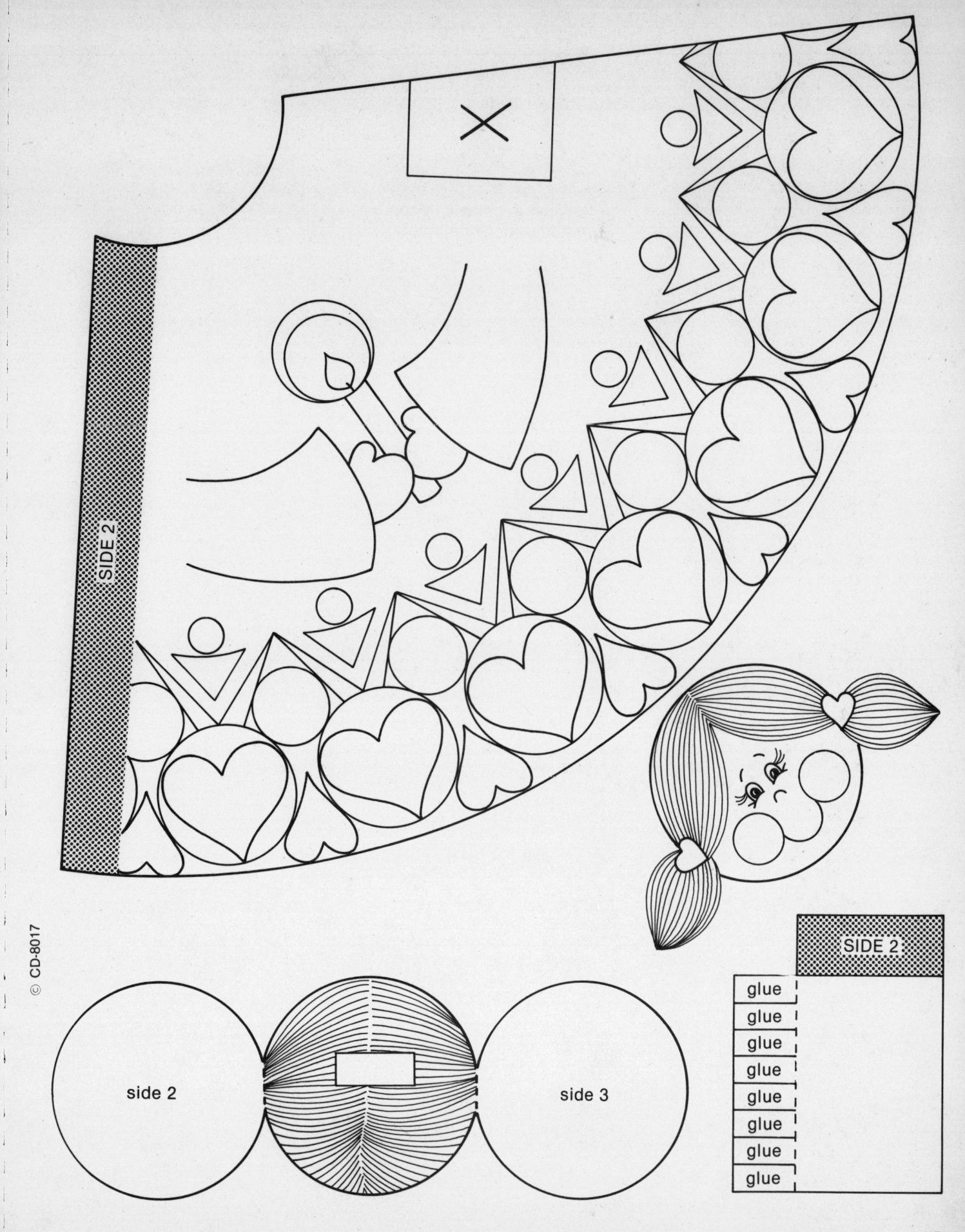

SIDE 2

side 2

side 3

SIDE 2

glue
glue
glue
glue
glue
glue
glue
glue

CD-8017

5

side 1

body

face

neck

head

SIDE 1

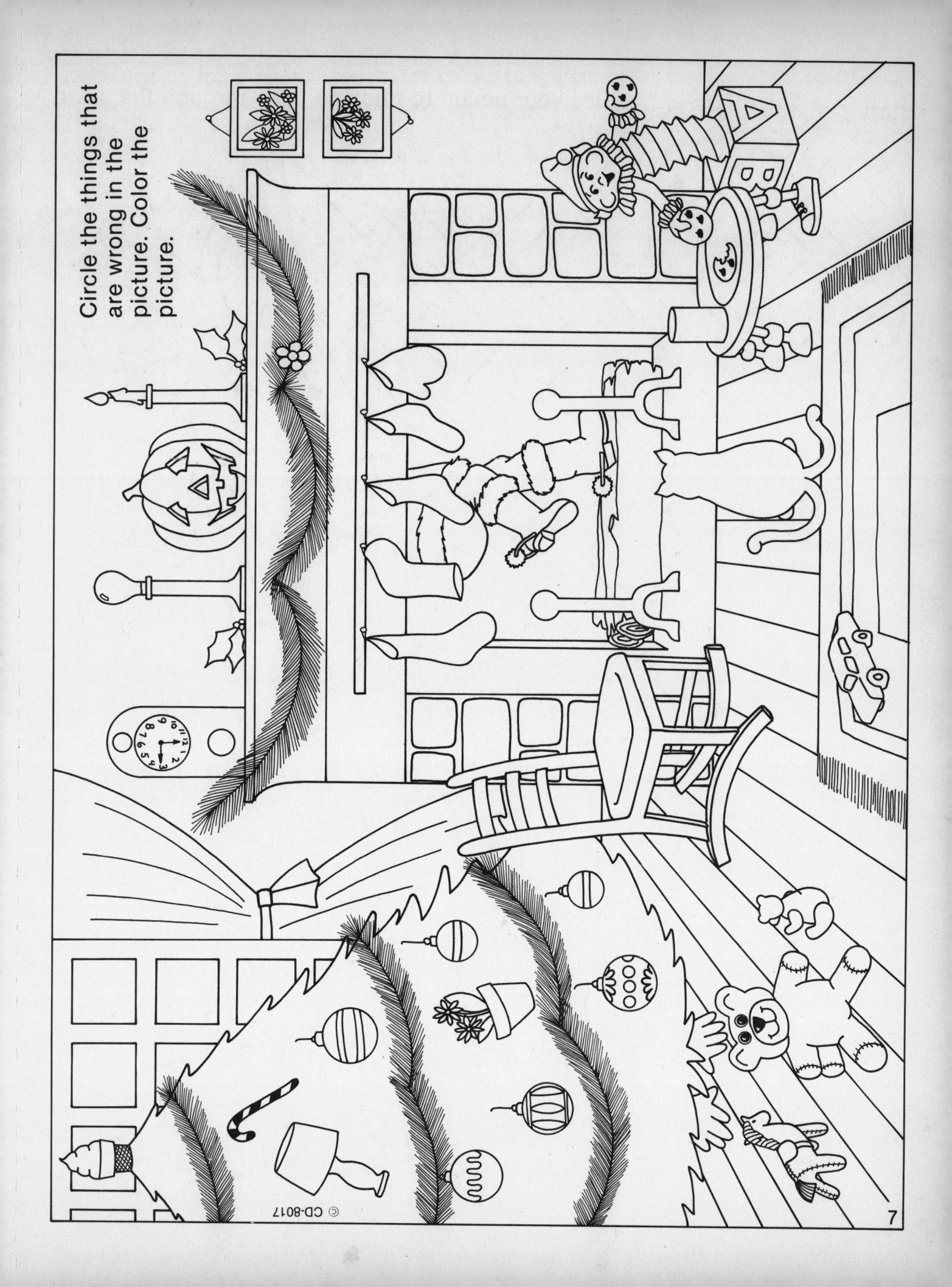

Circle the things that are wrong in the picture. Color the picture.

Start Use your pencil to find your way through the maze.

Finish

8

Christmas Gift Token

Give a very meaningful gift for Christmas by making a gift token stocking. On the back of each of the two candy canes, write a job or favor you'll do for the person to whom you're giving the stocking. Place the candy canes in the stocking and give the gift to a friend. Watch your friend's face beam with delight at your thoughtfulness!

Each pattern is labeled on the back. Cut on solid lines.

1. Color patterns.
2. Cut out patterns.
3. Fold stocking on dotted line.
4. Glue stocking together by placing glue on inside shaded edge of A. Glue A to B.

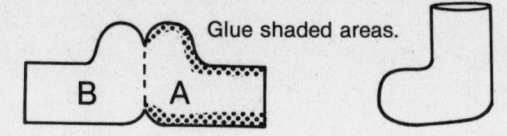

Glue shaded areas.

5. On the back of each candy cane, write a special favor you will do for the person to whom you will give the gift token stocking.
6. Insert candy canes in stocking.
7. Give stocking as a gift to a friend.

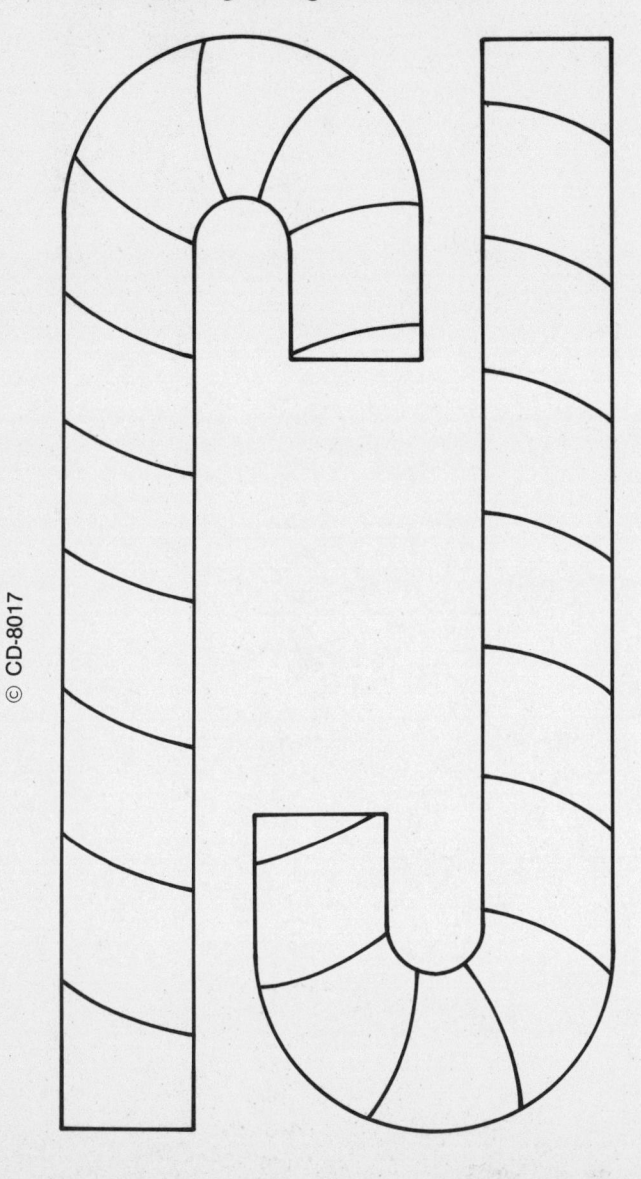

9

A

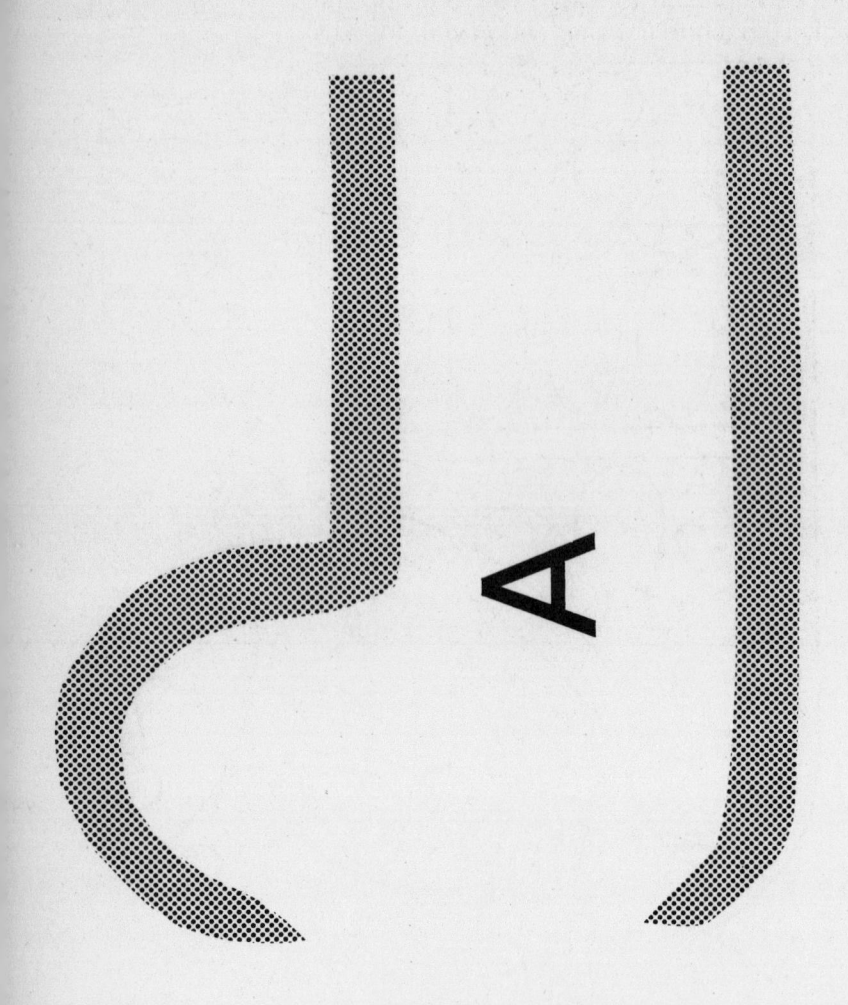

B

10

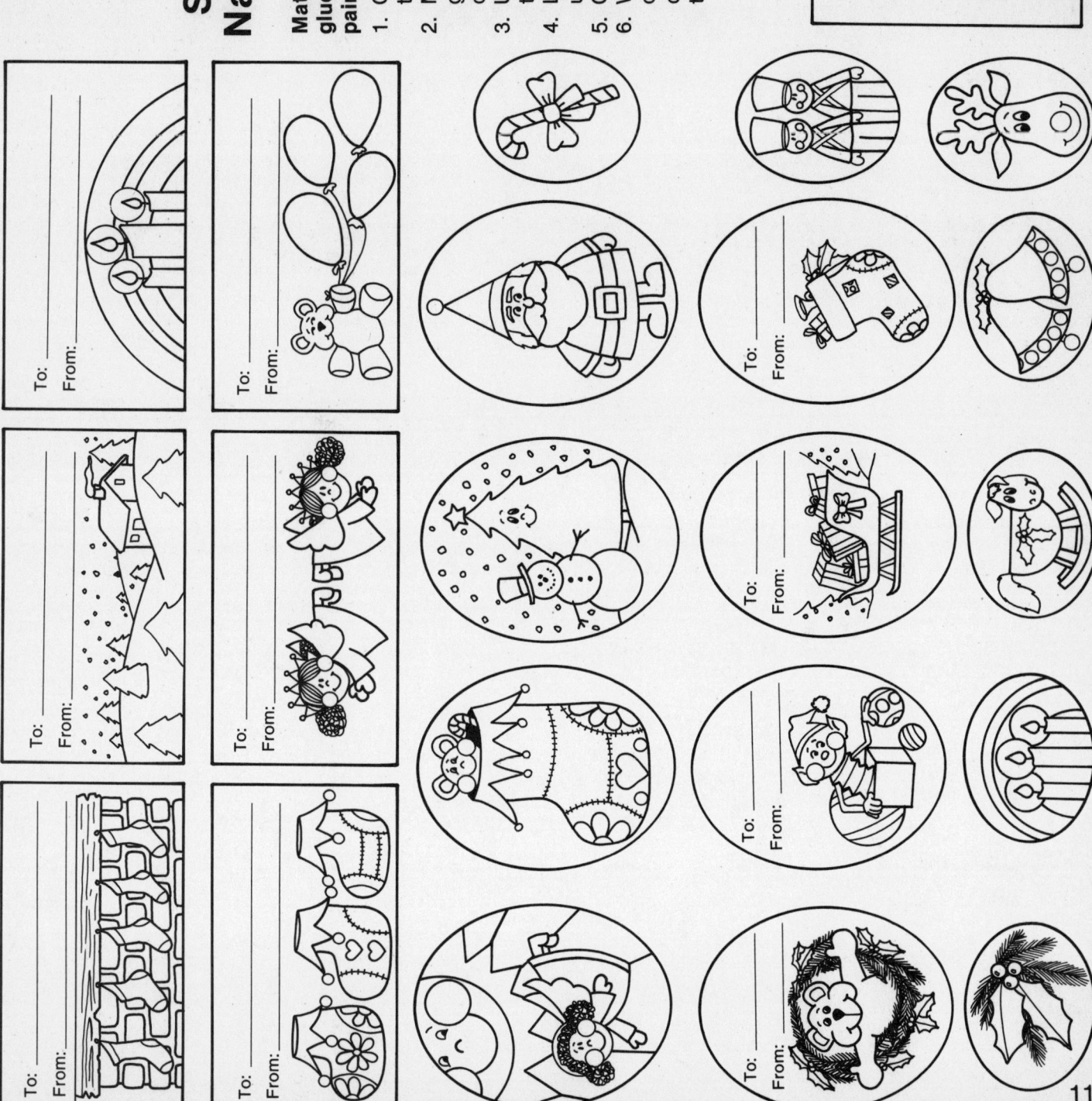

Stick-On Christmas Name Tags and Seals

Materials: crayons or markers, Lepages glue, scissors, water, water container, paintbrush.

1. Color each Christmas seal and name tag.
2. Mix an equal amount of Lepages glue and water together in a small container (paper cup).
3. Use a paintbrush to apply glue mixture to back of this page.
4. Let page dry completely, glue side up.
5. Cut out all name tags and seals.
6. When you are ready to use the seals or name tags, lick the back of each one or use a damp sponge and press to apply.

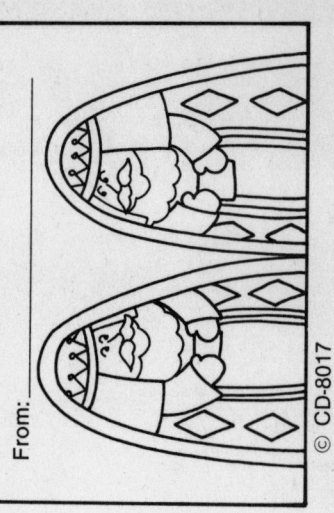

© CD-8017

11

Six Reindeer Napkin Holders

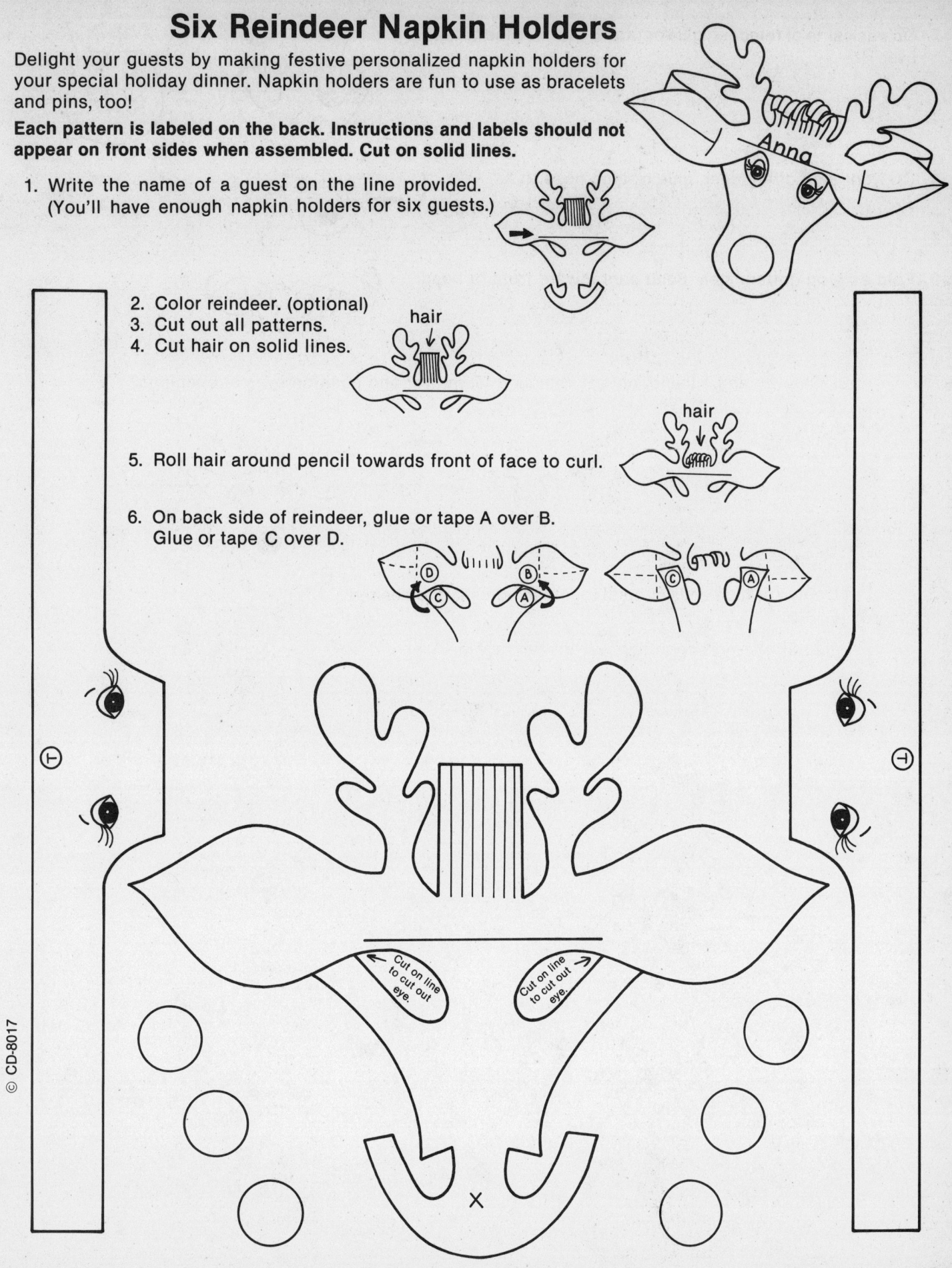

Delight your guests by making festive personalized napkin holders for your special holiday dinner. Napkin holders are fun to use as bracelets and pins, too!

Each pattern is labeled on the back. Instructions and labels should not appear on front sides when assembled. Cut on solid lines.

1. Write the name of a guest on the line provided. (You'll have enough napkin holders for six guests.)
2. Color reindeer. (optional)
3. Cut out all patterns.
4. Cut hair on solid lines.
5. Roll hair around pencil towards front of face to curl.
6. On back side of reindeer, glue or tape A over B. Glue or tape C over D.

CD-8017

12

7. On back side of reindeer, glue or tape E over F. Glue or tape G over H.

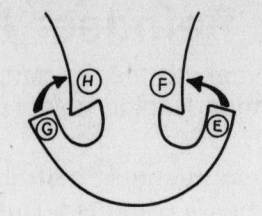

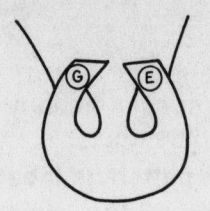

8. On front side of reindeer, glue or tape nose to X.

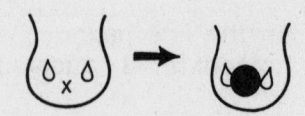

9. Fold ears on dotted lines. Bend ears toward front of head.

10. Glue or tape T (band) onto S (reindeer). Turn over and position eyes at openings.

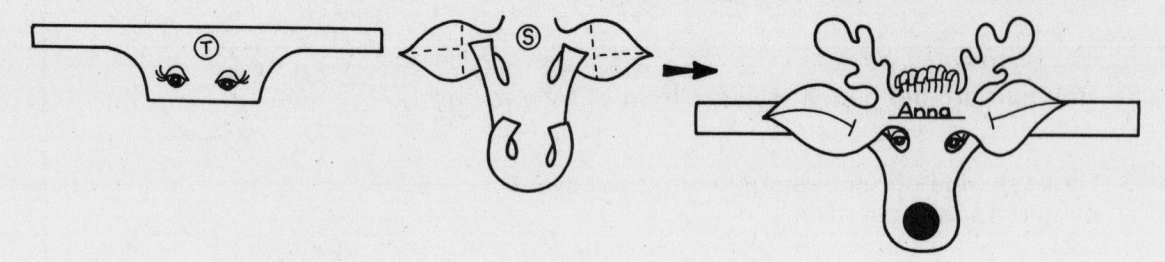

11. Glue or tape ends of band together, adjusting to desired size.

12. Slide reindeer holder over dinner napkin.

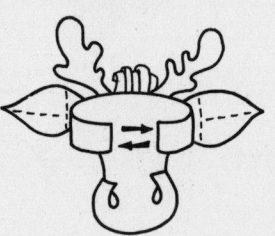

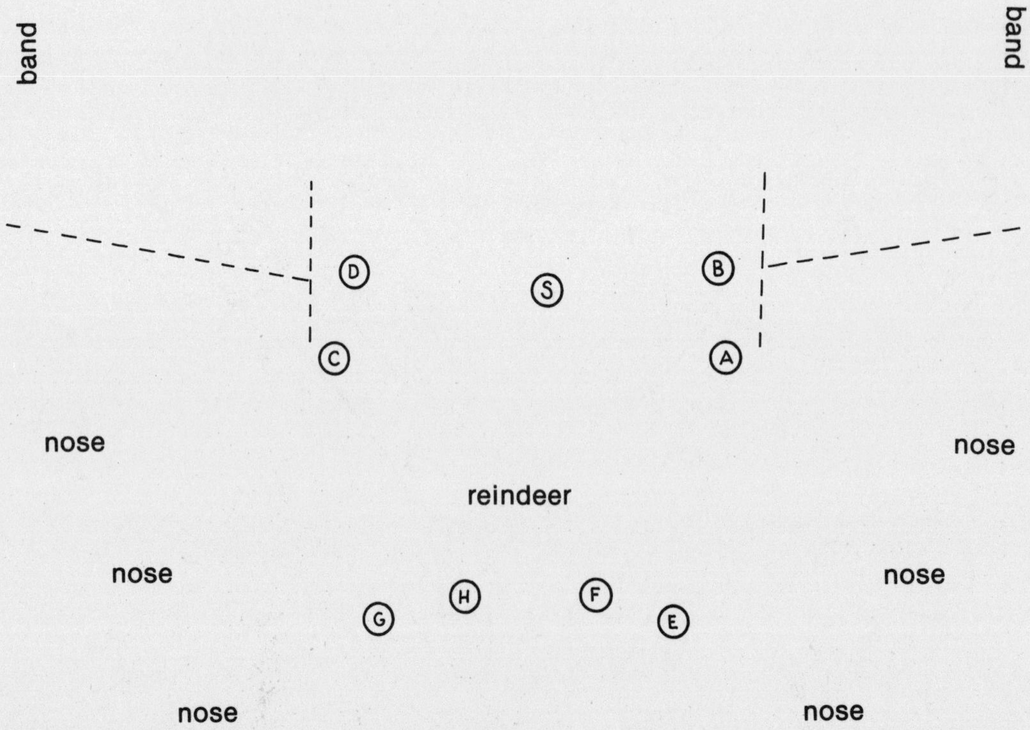

band

band

D S B
C   A

nose   nose

reindeer

nose   nose

G H F E

nose   nose

13

© CD-8017

Cut on line to cut out eye.

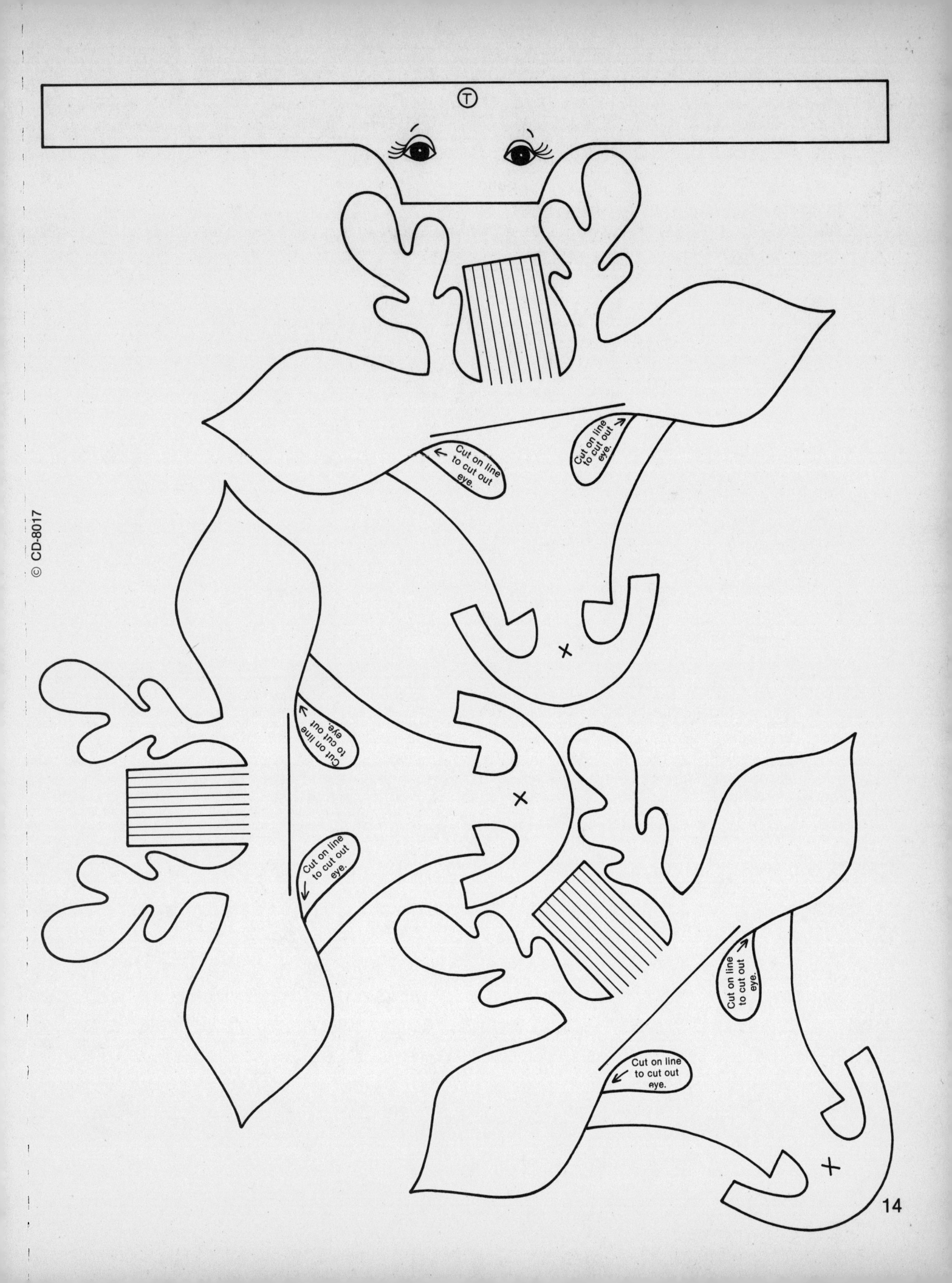

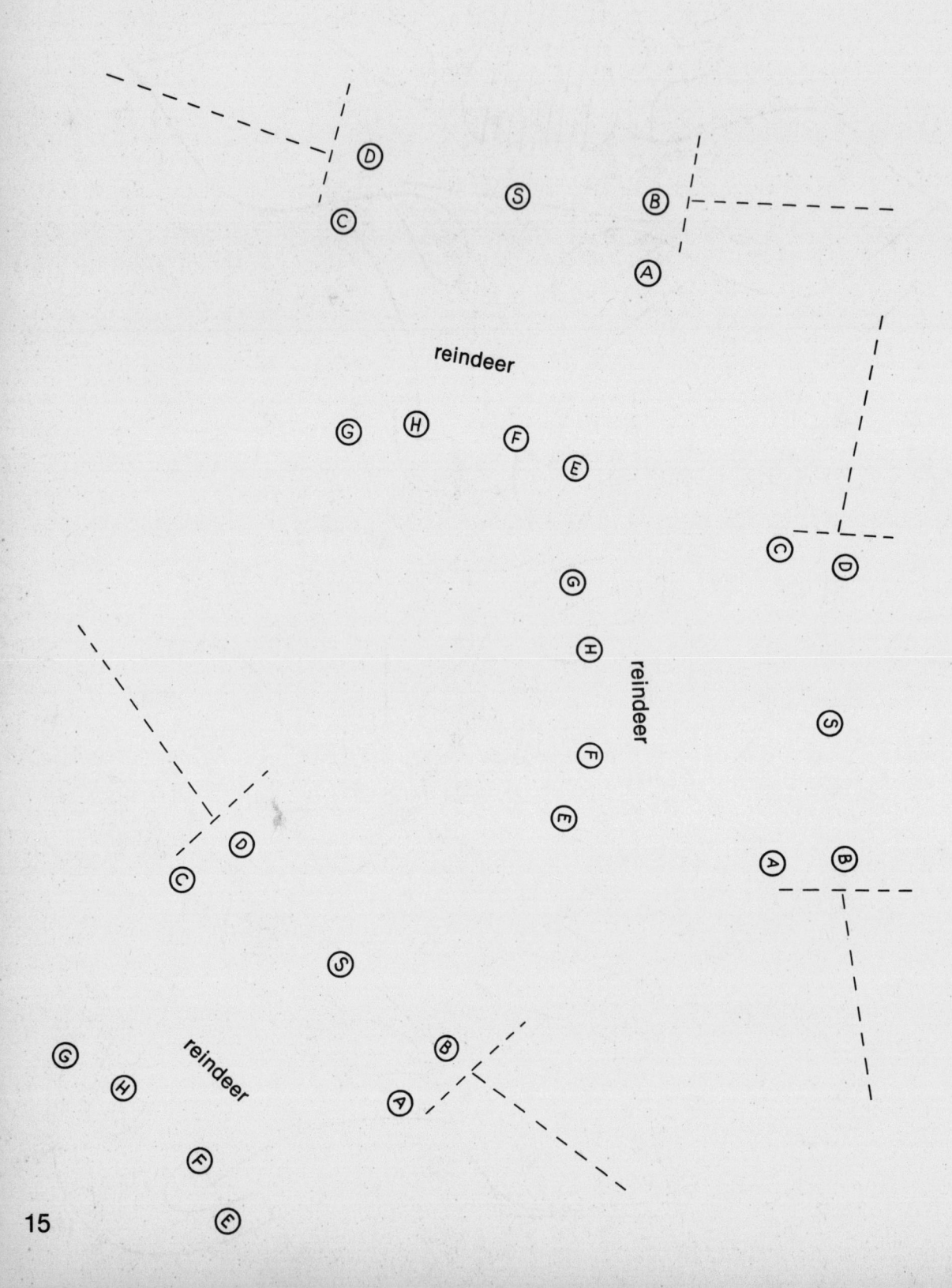

band

reindeer

reindeer

reindeer

Cut on line to cut out eye.   Cut on line to cut out eye.

Cut on line to cut out eye.   Cut on line to cut out eye.

CD-8017

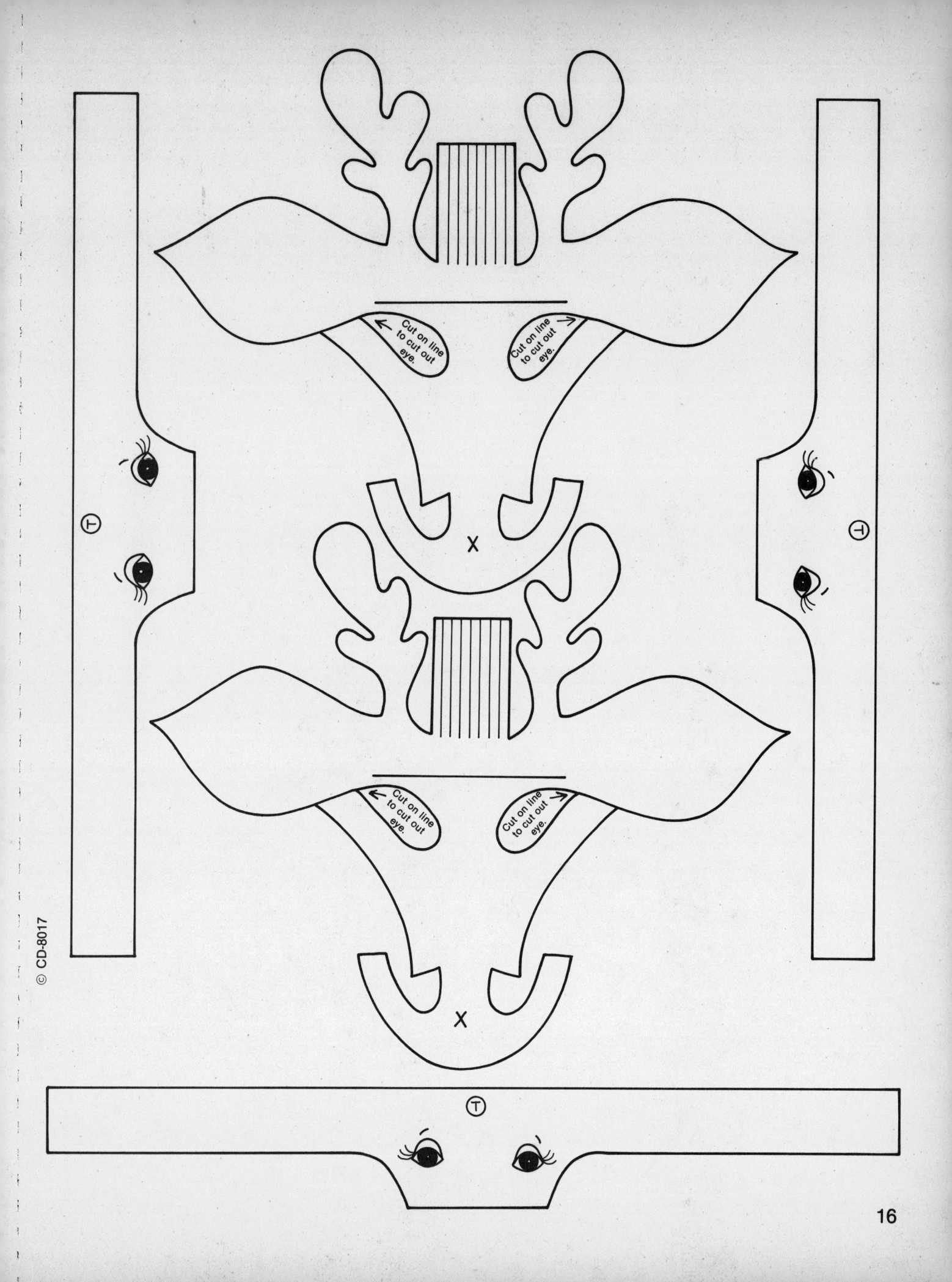

16

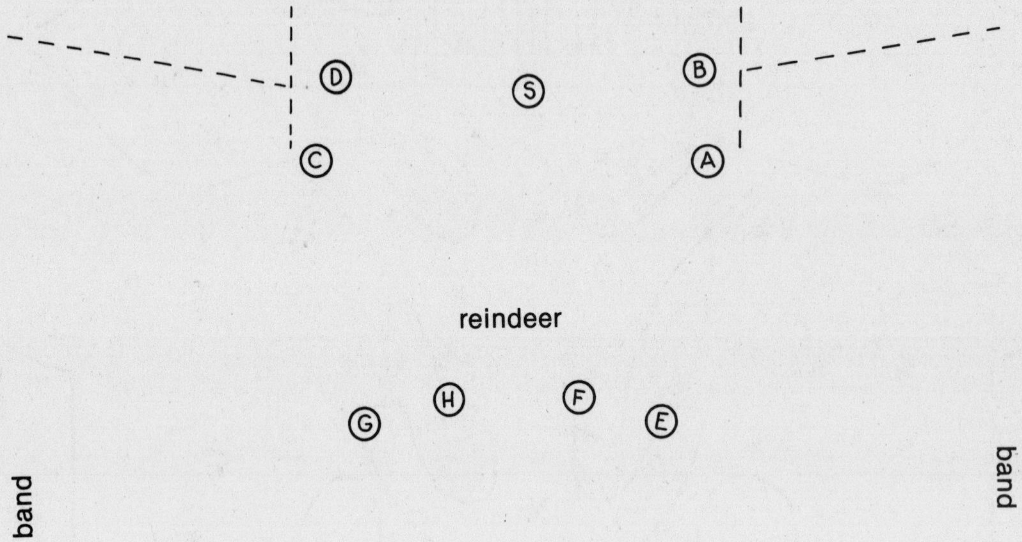

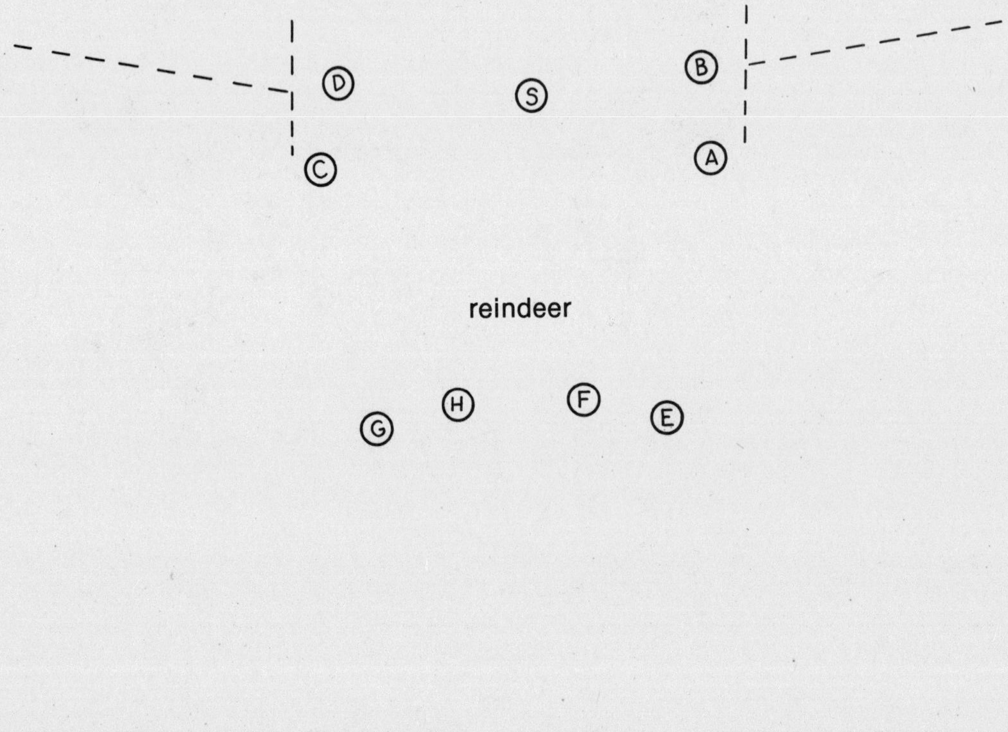

reindeer

band   band

reindeer

band

Christmas Word Search

Unscramble the words in the scrambled word list. Then locate the answers (unscrambled words) hidden in the puzzle. Circle the hidden words. The words are printed across and down and some words share a letter. An example has been done for you. Use the answer key to check your work.

SCRAMBLED WORD LIST

1. TNSRDCEOIAO DECORATIONS
2. HHMETEBLE _____
3. STILEN _____
4. SSMTARIHC REET _____
5. NTSIA LNHCAOSI _____
6. TLDEEIUY _____
7. LNGEA _____
8. TNNMRAEO _____
9. ESSUJ _____
10. LEON _____
11. REERENDI _____
12. HTWERA _____
13. YLIADHO _____
14. GLNROACI _____
15. AASTN _____
16. TPSEERSN _____
17. HLGSIE _____
18. HPRDLOU _____
19. TRSA _____
20. YTSO _____
21. DLGAANR _____
22. KTSSGNCOI _____
23. YMNCHIE _____
24. EIWS ENM _____
25. TTSLMIOEE _____
26. RMNGAE _____
27. GPPWNIAR _____

```
B E T H L E H E M Y D S R O P L
C H I M N E Y X T I N S E L O G
H I Q A D D U N C V G M O S R B
R T I N O E L Z W R E A T H N V
I J H G M N E S A A L W R T A M
S Y O E L L T R U I P S F K M T
T I L R U O I X N N E D C I E T
M P I F F P D W S A N T A C N J
A R D R G R E I N D E E R X T B
S E A U S T A R D F K I O A K A
T S Y D E O Q J E E K L L D E N
R E C O T Y Z N X M E P I G U G
E N S L I S F G A R L A N D T E
E T P P A S T O C K I N G S B L
C S T H O P S E K J E S U S F R
C S L E I G H Y W R A P P I N G
S A I N T N I C H O L A S D I A
W I S E M E N M I S T L E T O E
H (DECORATIONS) W O Q M
```

Answer Key: 1. DECORATIONS 2. BETHLEHEM 3. TINSEL 4. CHRISTMAS TREE 5. SAINT NICHOLAS 6. YULETIDE 7. ANGEL 8. ORNAMENT 9. JESUS 10. NOEL 11. REINDEER 12. WREATH 13. HOLIDAY 14. CAROLING 15. SANTA 16. PRESENTS 17. SLEIGH 18. RUDOLPH 19. STAR 20. TOYS 21. GARLAND 22. STOCKINGS 23. CHIMNEY 24. WISE MEN 25. MISTLETOE 26. MANGER 27. WRAPPING

Stained Glass Cookies

Have fun creating delicious tree ornaments! These cookies make fascinating decorations as well as tasty treats.

There are two methods to make the cookies. One method requires your imagination and strips of dough. The second method requires cookie cutters. In both cases, the center of each cookie is left open and filled with hard candy. When baked, stained glass cookies result!

Ingredients:
2 eggs
1 cup granulated sugar
¾ cup shortening (part butter or margarine, softened)
1 teaspoon almond extract
red or green food coloring (optional)
2½ cups all-purpose flour
1 teaspoon baking powder
1 teaspoon salt
¼ pound brightly colored candies (sour balls, lollipops, candy canes, etc.)

Materials:
- cookie dough
- aluminum foil
- colorful thread or yarn
- cookie cutters (optional)

Directions:

1. Blend eggs, sugar, shortening, almond extract and a few drops of red or green food coloring.
2. In another bowl, mix flour, baking powder and salt.
3. Stir second mixture into first mixture. Blend well.
4. Cover and chill for at least one hour.
5. Heat oven to 375°.
6. Roll dough to 1/8" thickness on lightly floured board.
7. Cut into thin strips (approximately ½" wide and 8" long).
8. Press strips into outline shapes such as angels, trees and stars. Leave centers open. (Create these shapes directly on aluminum foil on cookie sheet.)
9. Keep cookies about ½" apart on cookie sheet.
10. Cookie cutters can also be used to form shapes. (If cutters are used, be certain to remove center sections.)
11. With a toothpick, make a hole at the top of each cookie for hanging.
12. Crush candies and place into small bowls according to color.
13. Sprinkle crushed candies into open spaces, filling spaces evenly without piling candy.
14. Bake 7 to 9 minutes or until candy is melted and cookies are lightly browned.
15. Allow cookies to cool before removing them from foil.
16. Use brightly colored thread or yarn to hang cookies (or eat them!)

This recipe makes 6 dozen cookies.

Hand-Sewn Tree Ornaments

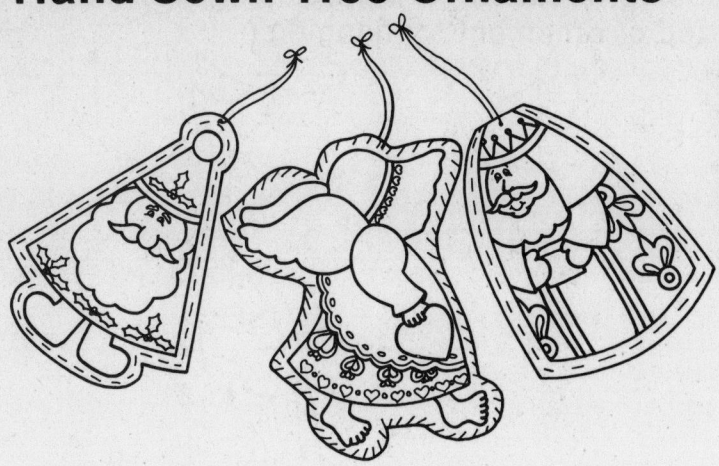

Show off your creative coloring and sewing skills by adding your special touch to these charming tree ornaments. You'll brighten everyone's holiday!

Materials: colored thread, needle, crayons or markers, scissors, tissue or shredded paper

1. Color ornaments brightly. If desired, add your own designs to ornaments.
2. Cut out all ornaments on heavy solid lines.
3. Fold ornament in half on dotted line.
4. Thread needle. Knot thread.
5. Sew together outer edges of ornament, making stitches same size. Leave an inch opening unsewn for stuffing. Do not cut or knot thread. 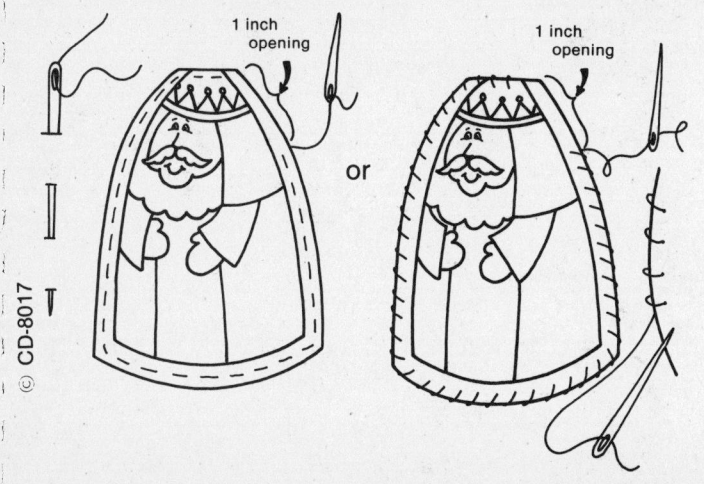
6. Stuff ornament with small pieces of facial tissue or shredded paper. Use a pencil to aid stuffing. Do not overstuff.

7. Sew opening closed and knot thread.
8. Using threaded needle, attach thread at top of ornament for hanging.

9. Hang ornament on tree or use to decorate house.

© CD-8017

22

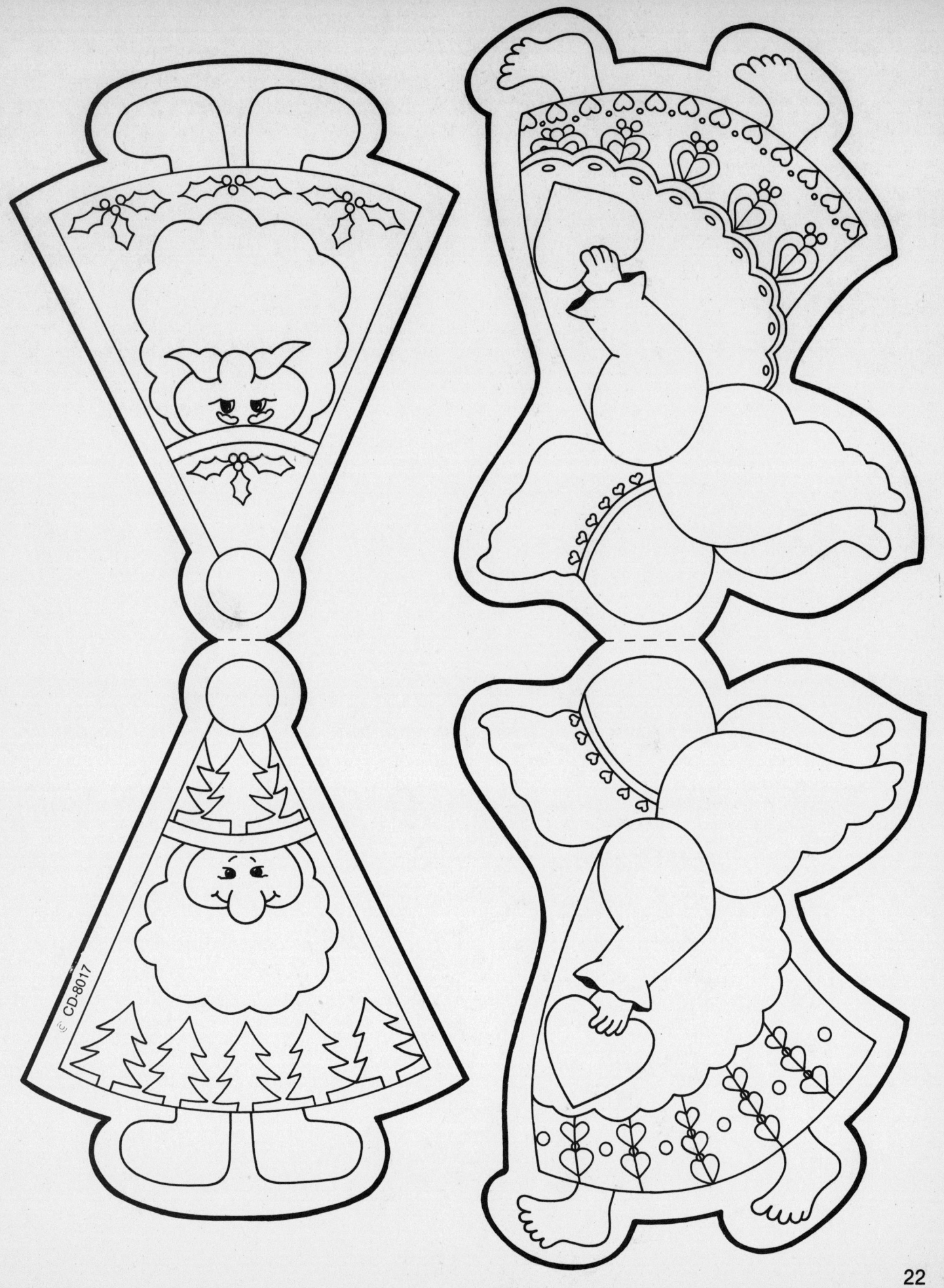

Santa-King Centerpiece
(Interchangeable)

The unique design of this centerpiece gives you the opportunity to view a face on both sides of the centerpiece. It can be seen and enjoyed fom all sides of a table. The hats are interchangeable, which makes it even more fun!

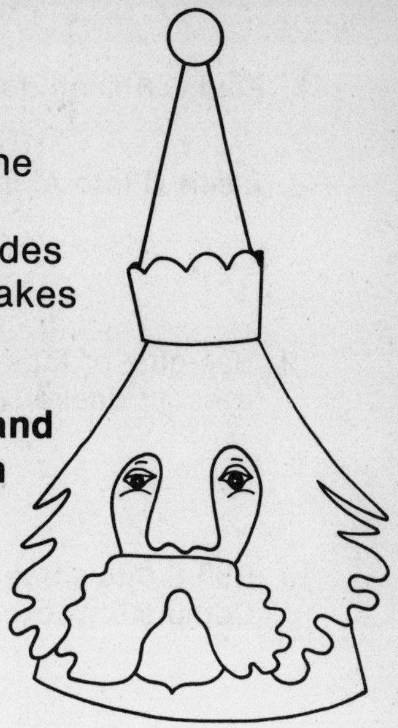

Each pattern is labeled on the back. Instructions and labels should not appear on outer sides when assembled. Cut on solid lines.

1. Color Santa's hat red (optional).
2. Color crown (optional).
3. Cut out all patterns.
4. Roll face and glue or tape side 1 over shaded area on side 2. Completely cover shaded area on side 2. 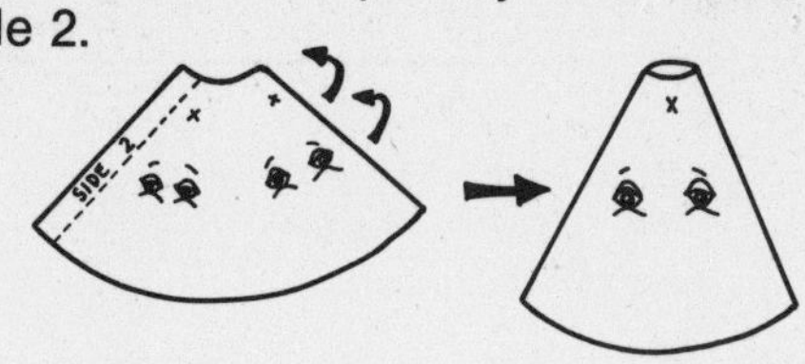
5. Fold A & B on dotted lines. 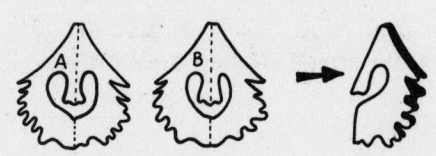
6. Cut slits on cut lines on A & B.

Use pen or pencil to punch hole, then cut with scissors.

© CD-8017

23

7. Fold C & D on dotted lines.

8. Insert C into A. Insert D into B. Make sure labels do not show on outer sides.

9. Use glue or tape to attach A to X (face). Attach B to Y (face). Center eyes. (If desired, place additional glue or tape at bottom of A and B.)

10. Roll Santa's hat and glue or tape side 1 over shaded area on side 2. Completely cover shaded area on side 2.

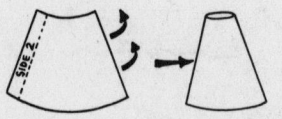

11. Glue or tape side 1 over shaded area on side 2 of Santa's hat trim. Completely cover shaded area on side 2.

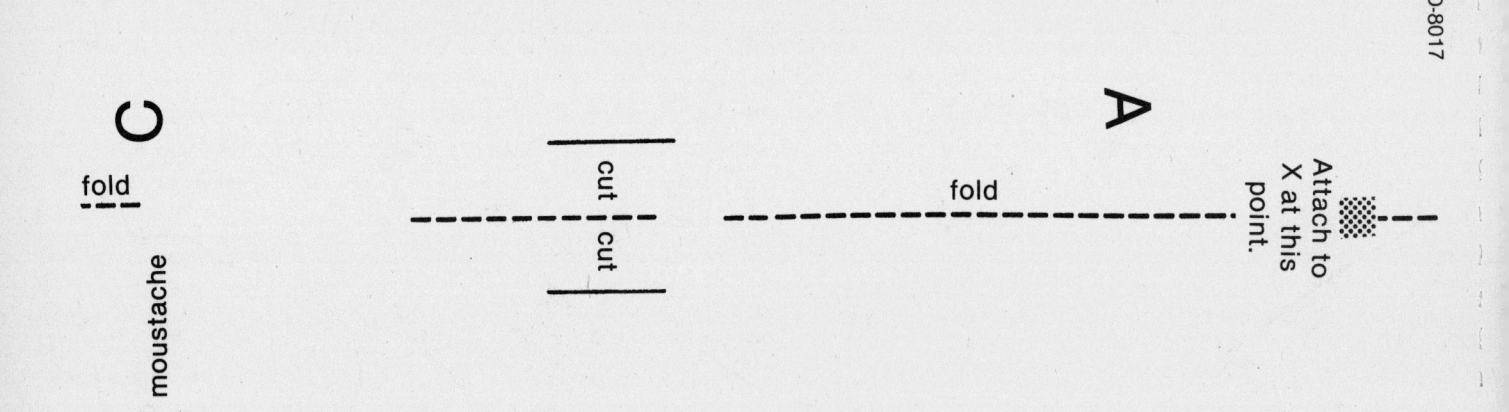

C
fold
moustache

cut
cut

A
fold
Attach to X at this point.

ball for hat

CD-8017

24

12. Slide hat trim over hat.

13. Insert ball into top of hat.

14. Glue or tape side 1 over shaded area on side 2 of crown. Completely cover shaded area on side 2.

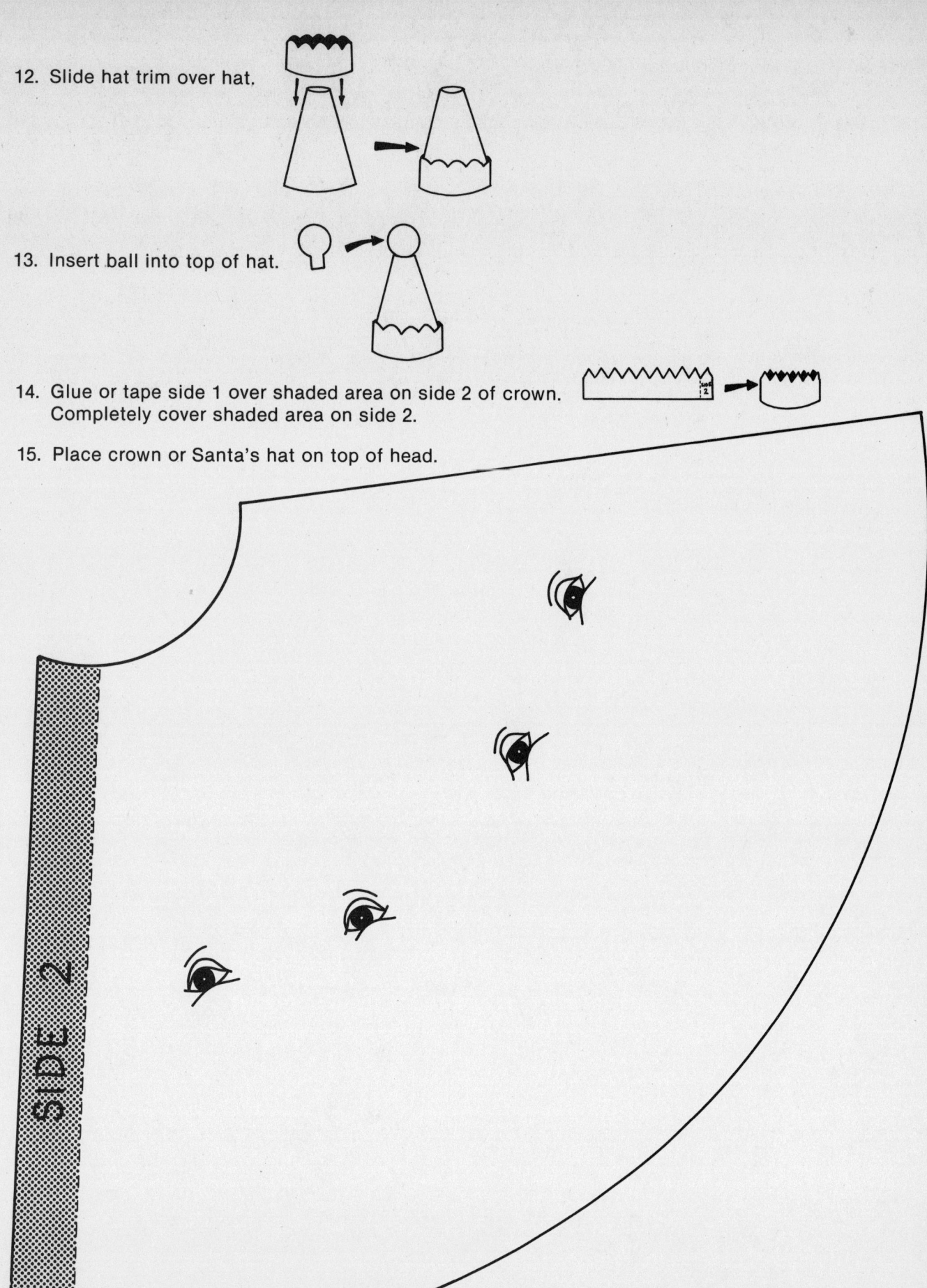

15. Place crown or Santa's hat on top of head.

SIDE 2

side 1

© CD-8017

X

face

Y

Use pen or pencil to punch hole, then cut with scissors.

SIDE 1

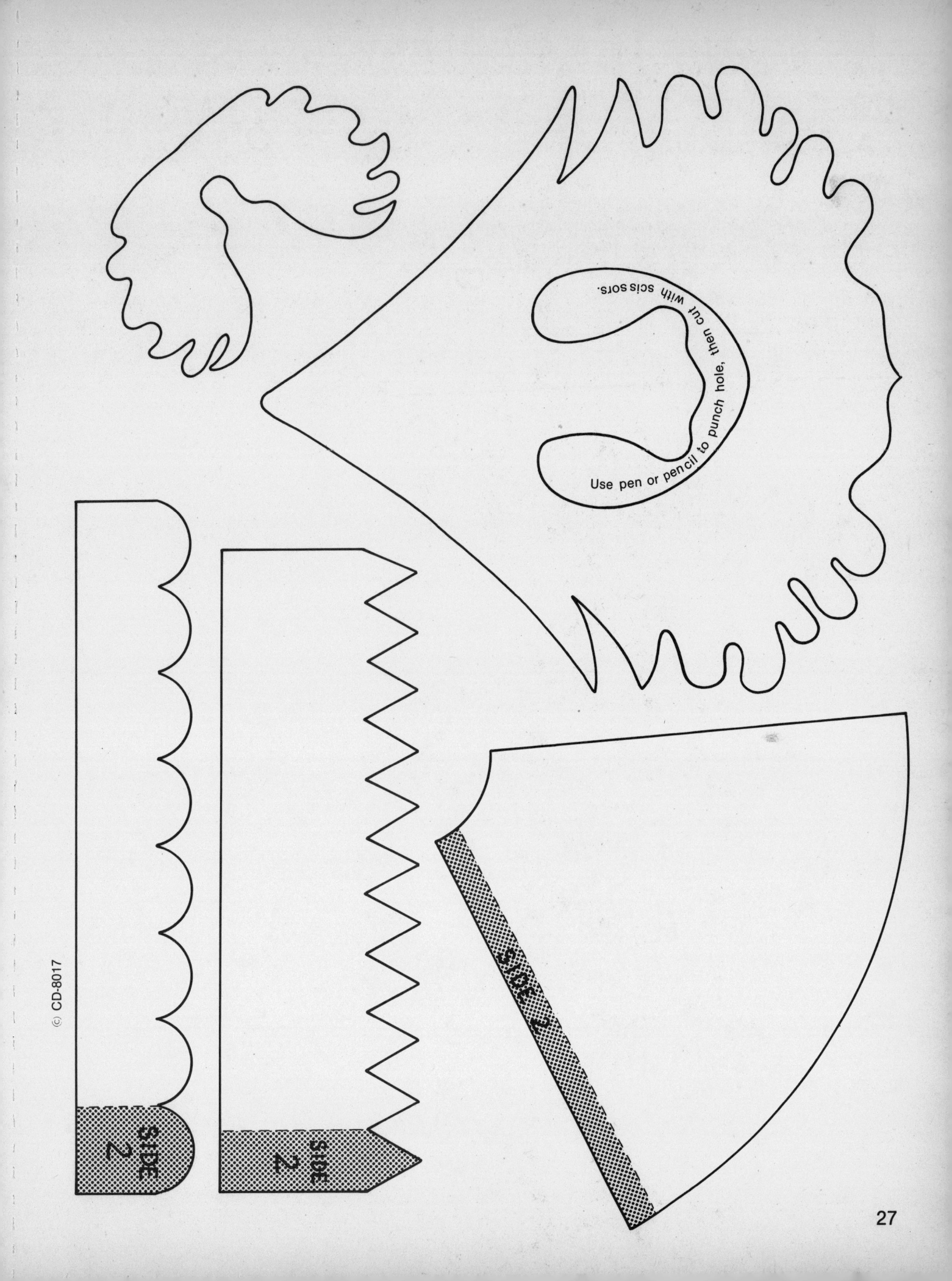

SIDE 2

SIDE 2

© CD-8017

27

D

fold

moustache

B

| cut
| cut

fold

Attach to Y at this point.

side 1

side 1

side 1

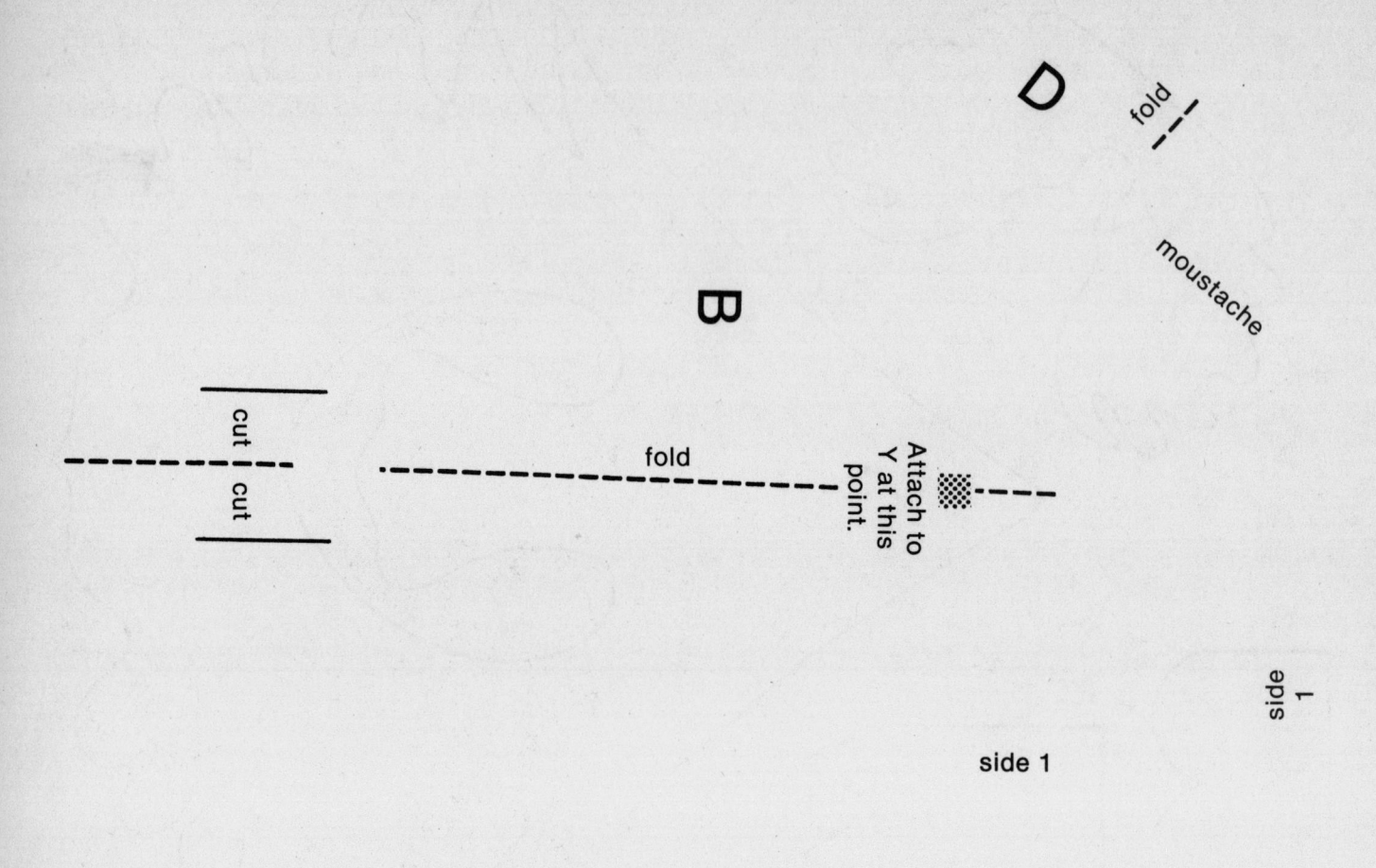

Santa's hat

crown

Santa's hat trim

28

© CD-8017

A Christmas Thank You Note

Directions: Color the card. Cut out the card on the heavy solid line. On the inside, fill in the name of the person to whom you will send the card. Write your thank you note, and sign your name. Address the front side of the card. Fold the card along the dotted lines. Paste or glue the seal. Add a stamp and mail!

From:

Place Stamp Here.

Front side of card

To:

Glue or paste seal here.

Inside of card

A Christmas Thank You

Dear _____,

_____

_____

_____

_____

_____,

_____

CD-8017